Reimagined

Reimagined

Embracing Change,
Celebrating New Beginnings.

Andre L. Mccloud

Copyright © 2025 Andre L McCloud

All rights reserved. No part of this publication may be reproduced, distributed or transmitted in any form or by any means, including photocopying, recording, or other electronic or mechanical methods, without the prior written permission of the publisher, except in the case of brief quotations embodied in critical reviews and certain other non-commercial uses permitted by copyright law.

Reimagined / Andre L. McCloud

DEDICATION

To my incredible wife Emily, thank you for your unwavering support and endless patience. Your belief in me has been my anchor, and I couldn't have come this far without you.

To my wonderful children, you fill my life with joy, wonder, and love. Your curiosity and resilience inspire me daily.

And to you, the reader, thank you for sharing in this journey. May these pages inspire you to pursue your dreams and embrace every step along the way.

With heartfelt gratitude,

Andre McCloud

"See, I am doing a new thing! Now it springs up; do you not perceive it? I am making a way in the wilderness and streams in the wasteland."

—Isaiah 43:19

CONTENTS

Welcome 1

Introduction 5

Section One: Reimagining Faith 7

Day 1. Reimagine Grace 8

Day 2. Reimagine Prayer 11

Day 3. Reimagine Trust 15

Day 4. Reimagine Surrender 18

Day 5. Reimagine Faithfulness 21

Day 6. Reimagine Perspective 24

Day 7. Reimagine Obedience 27

Day 8. Reimagine Joy 30

Section Two: Reimagining Purpose 33

Day 9. Reimagine Joy 34

Day 10. Reimagined Soervice 37

Day 11. Reimagined Stewardship 40

Day 12. Reimagined Work 44

Day 13. Reimagined Creativity 47

Day 14. Reimagined Leadership 50

Day 15. Reimagined Goals 53

Day 16. Reimagined Success 56

Section Three: Reimagining faithfulness 59

Day 17. Reimagined Patience 60

Day 18. Reimagined Resilience 63

Day 19 .Reimagined Trust...66

Day 20. Reimagined Discipline..69

Day 21. Reimagined Endurance...72

Day 22. Reimagined Hope 75

Day 23. Reimagined Healing..78

Day 24. Reimagined Forgivness 81

Section Four: Reimagining Love 85

Day 25. Reimagined Love for god 86

Day 26. Reimagined Love for Others 89

Day 27. Reimagined Compassion...92

Day 28. Reimagined Mercy 95

Day 29. Reimagined Sacrifice 98

Day 30. Reimagined Patience in Love 101

Day 31. Reimagined Pove for Enemies................................. 104

Day 32. Reimagined Unity in Love 107

Section Five: Reimagining the Future 111

Day 33. Reimagined Dreams.. 112

Day 34. Reimagined Purpose in Uncertainty....................... 115

Day 35. Reimagined Risk 118

Day 36. Reimagined Rest 121

Day 37. Reimagined Contentment....................................... 124

Day 38. Reimagined Conversations..................................... 127

Day 39. Reimagined Vision.. 130

Day 40. Reimagined Victory 133

WELCOME

Welcome to Reimagined: Embracing Change, Celebrating New Beginnings. Whether you're entering a season of new beginnings or simply sensing a call to refresh your faith, this devotional is here to guide you into deeper communion with God, encouraging you to see life through the lens of His transformative grace. Every day, we're given countless opportunities to grow, to deepen, and to see with new eyes what God is doing in our lives. Yet, embracing change can feel daunting, especially when we are accustomed to the familiar.

This devotional is designed to walk with you through 40 days of reflection, renewal, and a holy reimagining of life's possibilities in God's presence. As you journey through these days, you'll be invited to look at faith, purpose, and practice in fresh ways, to rekindle courage, and to approach life with the excitement and hope of someone stepping into something beautifully new.

EMBRACING CHANGE

Purpose of the Devotional

The purpose of this devotional is to equip you to welcome change, renew your heart, and cultivate a life that reflects the joy of God's unending promises. Each day presents an invitation to consider a different aspect of faith and life, from grace and trust to courage and love. Through this journey, we'll look at how God can "reimagine" even the most familiar parts of our faith, filling them with renewed purpose and meaning.

You'll find each day's reading to be short yet impactful, centered on Scripture and packed with real-life reflections. It's designed not only to deepen your relationship with God but also to prepare you to live out your faith in a world that is always changing.

How to Use This Devotional

1. Set Aside Time Daily: Each day's reflection can be read in a few minutes but try to give yourself 10-15 minutes to really absorb it. Allow God to speak through each passage, reflection, and prayer.

2. Engage with Scripture: Each day includes a Scripture passage to guide you. Take time to read and meditate on the verses, allowing the Word to illuminate the themes of each entry.

3. Reflect and Journal: This devotional includes space for notes and journaling. After each reading, spend a few moments reflecting on how God might be speaking to you personally. Writing down your thoughts, insights, and even your questions can deepen the journey.

4. Pray with Openness: End each reading with the prayer provided or offer up your own words to God. Prayer is essential in preparing your heart to embrace change and find new beginnings.

5. Invite the Holy Spirit: Transformation isn't a result of our efforts alone; it's a work of God in us. Before beginning each day, invite the Holy Spirit to open your heart and mind to what God wants to reveal.

Prayer for Openness

Heavenly Father, as I embark on this journey of reflection and renewal, I ask that You open my heart to Your presence. Give me the courage to embrace change and the grace to welcome new beginnings with joy and peace. Soften any resistance in me and fill my mind with Your wisdom. Guide me in seeing each step as part of Your divine purpose. Holy Spirit, be my teacher and companion as I walk through these days and help me reimagine my life in light of Your truth. In Jesus' name, I pray, Amen.

Let this journey be one of surrender and hope, filled with the reassurance that God's mercies are new every morning. You are ready, and God is with you. Let's begin this journey of reimagining life together.

INTRODUCTION

"See, I am doing a new thing! Now it springs up; do you not perceive it? I am making a way in the wilderness and streams in the wasteland."
— Isaiah 43:19

God is in the business of new beginnings. When He speaks through Isaiah, declaring, "I am doing a new thing," it's not just a promise for a distant future; it's an invitation for each of us to see and embrace the transformation He's unfolding right now. This passage reminds us that God is actively at work in places that seem dry, broken, or barren. Just as He brought water to the wilderness for His people, He brings renewal to our lives in the midst of change, guiding us to find beauty and purpose in what feels uncertain or even impossible.

To perceive this "new thing" that God is doing, we need fresh eyes and an open heart. Often, our familiarity with the past or fear of the unknown can cloud our vision, leaving us hesitant to step into the future He's designed. But Isaiah's words urge us to trust that God is leading us through every twist and turn, making paths where there were none and bringing life to places that seemed beyond hope. Embracing change is not easy, but it becomes possible when we realize that God goes before us, reimagining every part of our lives to align with His purpose and love.

As we journey through this devotional, let's lean into God's call to perceive the new things He is doing. Each day is an opportunity to reimagine aspects of our faith, our relationships, and our lives in light of His transformative grace. Just as God makes streams flow in the wasteland, He can bring life and growth to places in us that feel stagnant or weary. Together, let's embrace this season of renewal with hope and expectation, trusting that God's plans are far greater than what we can see.

SECTION ONE

REIMAGINING FAITH

Exploring fresh ways to connect with God, trust him, and deepen your spiritual foundation

DAY 1

REIMAGINED

GRACE

―――

"But he said to me, 'My grace is sufficient for you, for my power is made perfect in weakness.' Therefore, I will boast all the more gladly of my weaknesses, so that the power of Christ may rest upon me."
— 2 Corinthians 12:9

Paul was no stranger to hardship. Known for his tireless dedication to spreading the gospel, he faced prison, persecution, physical pain, and rejection. Yet, one struggle in particular seemed to haunt him, a "thorn in the flesh" that he begged God to remove. We don't know exactly what this thorn was, but it was severe enough that Paul prayed repeatedly for relief. Instead of taking away the difficulty, God gave him a deeper revelation: "My grace is sufficient for you, for my power is made perfect in weakness." Rather than an escape from his struggle, God offered Paul something far more profound, the assurance that His grace would sustain him through it.

This response may not have been what Paul expected, but it changed his entire perspective. He began to see his weakness not as a hindrance but as a stage for God's power to work. Reimagining grace means recognizing that God's favor doesn't just appear in our strengths or successes; it shows up most powerfully in our frailty, in those places where we feel least capable. Grace doesn't merely cover our past mistakes; it empowers us in the present, filling the gaps where we fall short. In Paul's case, this grace transformed his pain into a source of strength, reminding him daily that his life was dependent on God's sustaining power, not his own ability.

When we start to see grace in this way, it becomes a force that can transform every part of our lives. God's grace isn't just a free pass to try again when we mess up; it's a steady current that carries us, enabling us to keep going even when the path is hard. It's a power that lifts us up in our darkest hours and gives us the courage to face challenges that seem beyond us. Just as Paul learned to boast in his weakness because it magnified God's strength, we too can embrace our imperfections, knowing that God's grace meets us exactly where we are and does what we cannot do for ourselves.

Today, let's open our hearts to this reimagined understanding of grace, a grace that not only forgives but empowers, that doesn't eliminate our challenges but transforms them. Where are you feeling weak, inadequate, or burdened? God invites you to bring those areas to Him, trusting that His grace will carry you. You don't have to face these struggles alone; His power is ready to rest upon you, just as it did for Paul, bringing strength in your moments of deepest need.

Reflection Questions:

1. Where in your life do you feel weak or insufficient, and how might God be inviting you to experience His grace in that area?

2. How does understanding grace as an empowering force, rather than just forgiveness, change the way you approach challenges in your life?

DAY 2

REIMAGINED

PRAYER

Rejoice always, pray without ceasing, give thanks in all circumstances; for this is the will of God in Christ Jesus for you.
- 1 Thessalonians 5:16-18

For many of us, prayer can become something we turn to mainly in moments of need or crisis, a ritual we perform when we need guidance or a solution. But in his letter to the Thessalonians, Paul urges believers to "pray without ceasing," suggesting that prayer is intended to be more than an occasional activity; it's meant to be a constant, living connection with God. Reimagining prayer means seeing it as an ongoing relationship rather than just an isolated practice. It's a lifestyle of inviting God into every moment, a continual awareness of His presence that transforms the way we live and see the world.

Imagine if prayer wasn't something we checked off a list but was more like breathing, a natural, continual part of our day. Think about the small, daily routines: washing dishes, commuting, waiting in line. These ordinary moments can become invitations for simple prayers of gratitude, surrender, or trust. Whispering a quick "thank you" for your family while making breakfast or asking for God's guidance on a work project as you start your day, can transform everyday tasks into sacred moments. This is the essence of "praying without ceasing", keeping a steady flow of conversation and connection with God in the middle of our routines.

When prayer becomes a way of life, our connection with God deepens in unexpected ways. We may find ourselves more aware of His comfort when stress arises, or more attuned to His wisdom when making decisions. This shift allows us to experience God as not just a distant authority but a close companion. Instead of waiting for our "prayer time" to address concerns or express gratitude, we can bring our needs, worries, and joys to God moment by moment, knowing He is always present and listening. Even a quick breath prayer, a few words spoken in your heart, can remind you that God is near and cares about every detail of your day.

In this way, prayer becomes a powerful tool for cultivating peace and grounding ourselves in God's presence, even in the busiest seasons. You might find that the pressures of life feel lighter when you're in regular conversation with God, or that frustration eases when you lift it to Him in a quick prayer. By reimagining prayer as an ongoing dialogue, we become more resilient, knowing that we don't have to face any moment alone. This continual connection with God equips us to navigate the highs and lows of life with a spirit of gratitude and joy, trusting that He is at work in all things, big and small.

Today, as you go through your routines, consider how you might make space for "unceasing prayer" in the small pauses and transitions of your day. Let each moment be an opportunity to tune your heart to God's presence and to share your thoughts, needs, and thankfulness with Him. Through this habit, prayer will become the steady rhythm of your life, a source of strength, comfort, and joy no matter what you face.

Reflection Questions:

1. In what everyday moments could you start inviting God's presence through simple, quick prayers?

2. How could viewing prayer as a continual, two-way conversation with God change your approach to the day's challenges and decisions?

3. What difference do you think it would make in your life if you made space for "breath prayers" or quiet gratitude throughout the day?

4. How might regular, ongoing prayer affect your relationships, mindset, and sense of peace?

DAY 3

Reimagined

TRUST

"Trust in the lord with all your heart, and do not lean on your own understanding. in all your ways acknowledge him, and he will make straight your paths."
— Proverbs 3:5-6

Trust is at the core of our relationship with God, yet it's often one of the hardest things to fully embrace. Proverbs 3:5-6 reminds us to "trust in the Lord with all your heart," urging us to rely on His wisdom rather than our own understanding. This is easier said than done, especially when life feels unpredictable or when our plans don't align with God's. Trusting God means believing that His perspective is infinitely greater than ours, even when the path ahead seems unclear. It's about releasing control and leaning into the One who holds all things in His hands.

Reimagining trust challenges us to move beyond a surface-level faith. Instead of simply believing in God's power, we are invited to actively rely on it. This trust isn't passive; it requires an ongoing relationship with Him. Trusting God means inviting Him into every decision, every fear, and every hope, allowing His guidance to shape our steps. As we acknowledge Him in all our ways, no matter how small or significant, He promises to direct our paths. This doesn't mean the road will always be smooth, but it will lead to His best for us.

When we face uncertainty, it's natural to rely on our own understanding, trying to figure things out in our strength. But reimagined trust requires us to let go of this tendency and instead turn to God's Word and His Spirit for direction. Trusting Him doesn't mean we ignore our responsibilities or dismiss wise counsel; it means we place our confidence in His overarching plan. It's a daily act of faith to say, "Lord, I don't see how this will work out, but I trust You to guide me."

In practical terms, trusting God might look like surrendering control in a specific area of life, such as your career, relationships, or finances. It could mean choosing peace over worry, praying before making a big decision, or taking a step of faith when the outcome is uncertain. Trust isn't about having all the answers; it's about knowing the One who does. This kind of trust not only brings peace but also frees us from the weight of trying to manage everything on our own.

Take a moment today to identify areas in your life where you find it difficult to trust God. What burdens are you carrying that He is asking you to release? Trusting Him doesn't guarantee instant solutions, but it does promise His presence, peace, and direction. Reimagined trust is a partnership, leaning on Him every step of the way and believing He will make your paths straight, even when the road ahead seems uncertain.

Reflection Questions:

1. What is one area of your life where you struggle to trust God?

2. What might it look like to surrender this area to Him?

3. How does trusting in your own understanding impact your peace and decision-making?

4. What steps can you take to acknowledge God in your daily routines and decisions?

DAY 4

REIMAGINED
SURRENDER

~~~

"And He said to all, 'If anyone would come after me, let him deny himself and take up his cross daily and follow me.'"
— Luke 9:23

Surrender is a word that often feels uncomfortable. It challenges our natural desire for control, asking us to release our plans, desires, and expectations into God's hands. In Luke 9:23, Jesus calls His followers to deny themselves, take up their crosses daily, and follow Him. This is not just a one-time decision but a daily choice to surrender our will and align our lives with God's purpose. Reimagining surrender helps us see it not as a loss, but as an act of faith that leads to true freedom.

To surrender is to let go of the need to dictate every outcome and instead trust in God's infinite wisdom and goodness. This can feel risky because it requires us to relinquish control, but it is in surrender that we find peace. When we try to hold on too tightly to our own plans, we can become burdened by stress and disappointment. But when we trust God's purpose, we find relief in knowing that He is working for our good, even in ways we cannot see. Surrender becomes an act of trust, allowing God to take the lead and direct our steps.

Reimagined surrender doesn't mean giving up responsibility or becoming passive. Instead, it calls us to actively align our desires with God's will. It's about asking, "Lord, what do You want for my life?" and being willing to follow His direction, even when it's challenging or unexpected. Taking up our cross daily reminds us that surrender is not always comfortable, it requires humility and perseverance. Yet, it also brings the joy of walking in step with God's plan, which is always better than anything we could create on our own.

In our everyday lives, surrender might look like releasing control over situations we can't change or choosing to obey God in areas where we feel hesitant. It could mean trusting Him with a career decision, a strained relationship, or an uncertain future. When we surrender, we open ourselves to the possibilities of what God can do through us and for us. His plans are far greater than our own, and His timing is always perfect. By surrendering, we invite His power and purpose to shape our lives in ways we never imagined.

Take time today to reflect on areas of your life where surrender feels difficult. What are you holding onto that God is asking you to release? Surrender is not about losing; it's about gaining the fullness of life that God has planned for you. As you take up your cross and follow Him, you'll discover the freedom that comes from trusting Him completely.

Reflection Questions:

1. What does surrendering your will and desires to God mean to you personally?

2. What areas of your life are hardest for you to release control over? Why?

3. How can taking up your cross daily help you trust God's purpose for your life?

4. Can you recall a time when surrendering to God's plan brought unexpected peace or blessing?

DAY 5

Reimagined
FAITHFULNESS

"The steadfast love of the Lord never ceases; His mercies never come to an end; they are new every morning; great is Your faithfulness."
– Lamentations 3:22-23

Faithfulness is a cornerstone of God's character. In Lamentations 3:22-23, we are reminded of His steadfast love and unending mercy. Even in the midst of hardship, God's faithfulness never wavers. Each day, His mercies are renewed, offering us a fresh start and the reassurance that He is with us. Reimagining faithfulness begins by reflecting on the consistency of God's love, a love that holds us steady through every trial and triumph. It is His faithfulness that inspires and sustains our own commitment to Him.

God's faithfulness is not dependent on our circumstances or even our actions. Whether we are walking closely with Him or stumbling through a season of doubt, His love remains constant. This unwavering nature invites us to trust Him completely, knowing He will never leave or forsake us. When we take time to reflect on the ways God has been faithful in our lives, providing, protecting, and guiding, we are reminded of His unchanging goodness and are encouraged to remain faithful in return.

Reimagined faithfulness also challenges us to model God's steadfast love in our own lives. Just as He is faithful to us, we are called to remain steadfast in our faith, even when it's difficult. This might mean holding onto hope when prayers go unanswered, staying committed to His Word in seasons of busyness, or trusting His timing when life feels uncertain. Faithfulness is not just a passive state of being; it's an active choice to follow God's path, day by day, regardless of what we face.

In daily life, faithfulness can look like small, consistent acts of devotion, spending time in prayer, studying Scripture, or serving others. It's about showing up for God and allowing Him to shape our character over time. Faithfulness is cultivated not through perfection but through persistence, choosing to stay connected to God even in our struggles. Each time we take a step of faith, no matter how small, we reflect His own steadfast love back to Him.

Take a moment today to reflect on God's faithfulness in your life. Where have you seen His unchanging love, even in difficult times? Allow these reminders to renew your commitment to remain faithful in your own journey with Him. Faithfulness isn't about never faltering; it's about continually turning back to the One whose mercies are new every morning. In His faithfulness, we find the strength and courage to persevere.

Reflection Questions:

1. How has God's faithfulness been evident in your life, even during challenging seasons?

2. What does it mean for you to reflect God's faithfulness in your own daily walk?

3. Are there areas where you struggle to remain steadfast in your faith?

4. How can remembering God's faithfulness help you?

DAY 6

REIMAGINED
PERSPECTIVE

"Do not be conformed to this world, but be transformed by the renewal of your mind, that by testing you may discern what is the will of God, what is good and acceptable and perfect."
— Romans 12:2

Perspective shapes how we view every aspect of life. Romans 12:2 challenges us to move beyond the patterns of this world and to let God transform our minds. This transformation isn't about small tweaks; it's about seeing the world through God's eyes. Reimagining perspective means shifting from a limited, human-centered view to one that is rooted in His eternal truth. When we allow God to renew our minds, our faith deepens, and we begin to approach life with clarity and purpose that only He can provide.

Conforming to the world's perspective often leads to discouragement, comparison, and misplaced priorities. The world teaches us to value success, status, and comfort above all else, but God's perspective calls us to something greater. Reimagining perspective means recognizing that God's ways are higher than ours and that His plans are always for our good. It allows us to see beyond the temporary and focus on what truly matters: loving God, serving others, and walking in obedience to His will.

This shift in perspective doesn't happen automatically, it requires intentionality. We need to spend time in God's Word, letting His truth shape our thinking and challenge the lies we may have believed. It's through Scripture and prayer that we begin to align our thoughts with God's heart. As our perspective changes, so do our actions. We start to live with a sense of hope and purpose, even in difficult seasons, because we see our circumstances in light of God's eternal promises.

Reimagined perspective also changes how we view ourselves and others. When we see ourselves as God's beloved children we are freed from striving for approval or perfection. And when we view others through His eyes, we're more likely to extend grace, compassion, and love. This renewed perspective helps us to focus less on what divides us and more on the unity we share in Christ. It enables us to live with greater kindness and generosity, reflecting God's love in our daily interactions.

Today, ask God to help you see the world through His eyes. Where do you need a renewed perspective? Whether it's how you view your challenges, your relationships, or your purpose, invite Him to transform your mind. As you walk in this reimagined perspective, you'll find that your faith deepens, your hope grows, and your life is increasingly aligned with God's perfect will.

Reflection Questions:

1. In what areas of your life have you been conforming to the world's perspective instead of God's?

2. How can spending time in God's Word help you reimagine your perspective and align it with His truth?

3. How does seeing yourself as God's beloved child change the way you approach your daily life?

4. What steps can you take to view others with greater compassion and love, reflecting God's perspective in your relationships?

DAY 7

Reimagined

OBEDIENCE

~~~

"If you love me, you will keep my commandments."
— John 14:15

Obedience is often misunderstood as a rigid set of rules we must follow to earn God's favor. But Jesus reframes obedience in John 14:15, showing us that it is rooted in love. When we love God, obedience becomes a natural response, a way of expressing our trust in His wisdom and care for us. Reimagining obedience means moving beyond obligation and seeing it as an act of devotion, where our actions reflect our relationship with God and our desire to honor Him.

Obedience can feel burdensome when we focus solely on what we must give up. But when we trust that God's commands are given out of His love for us, obedience becomes freeing. His ways are always for our good, leading us toward a life that aligns with His purpose and blessings. When we reimagine obedience, we see it not as something restrictive, but as the pathway to peace, joy, and fulfillment in Him. It's about choosing His will because we believe He knows what is best for us, even when we don't fully understand.

In daily life, obedience often involves small, quiet decisions, choosing honesty in a difficult situation, forgiving when it's hard, or stepping out in faith when we feel afraid. These moments may seem insignificant, but they are opportunities to show our love for God and trust in His plan. Reimagining obedience reminds us that every act of faithfulness, no matter how small, draws us closer to Him and allows His work to be evident in our lives.

Obedience also deepens our relationship with God. When we choose to follow His commands, we experience His presence in profound ways. As we align our lives with His Word, we begin to see the beauty of His design and the blessings that come from living according to His will. Obedience is not about perfection, it's about surrender, acknowledging our dependence on Him and allowing His Spirit to guide and strengthen us each day.

Take a moment to reflect on how you view obedience. Is it something you approach with reluctance or love? Reimagined obedience invites us to embrace God's commands with a heart of trust and gratitude, knowing that He is leading us toward the fullness of life He has prepared. When we obey out of love, our actions become a reflection of our faith and a testimony of His goodness.

Reflection Questions:

1. How does viewing obedience as an act of love rather than an obligation change your perspective?

2. What areas of your life is God calling you to greater obedience? How can you trust Him in these areas?

3. Can you recall a time when following God's commands brought unexpected peace or blessing? How did it deepen your faith?

4. How can you incorporate small, daily acts of obedience into your life as a way of expressing your love for God?

DAY 8

REIMAGINED

JOY

~~~

*"Do not grieve, for the joy of the
Lord is your strength."*
— Nehemiah 8:10

Joy is often misunderstood as a fleeting emotion tied to our circumstances. But in Nehemiah 8:10, we are reminded that the joy of the Lord is something far deeper, a source of strength that sustains us even in life's most difficult moments. Reimagining joy means shifting our focus from temporary happiness to the enduring joy that comes from knowing and trusting God. It is a joy that transcends challenges, rooted in His presence and promises.

This joy is not dependent on everything going right in our lives. In the context of Nehemiah, the Israelites had just returned from exile and were rebuilding their lives. Though they faced struggles and uncertainty, they were reminded to rejoice in the Lord, for His faithfulness remained. Reimagining joy invites us to find strength in God's unchanging character, rather than in the ups and downs of life. It's a joy that grows from a vibrant relationship with Him, where we trust in His love and His purpose for us.

In daily life, reimagined joy might look like finding reasons to be thankful even when circumstances feel overwhelming. It could be pausing to recognize God's blessings, a kind word from a friend, the beauty of creation, or the quiet assurance of His presence. Joy doesn't mean ignoring pain or pretending everything is perfect; it means choosing to celebrate God's goodness in the midst of it all. It's a defiant declaration that His joy is greater than our trials.

This kind of joy also strengthens us for the journey. When we lean into the joy of the Lord, we find the energy and hope to keep going, even when the road is hard. It lifts our eyes above the challenges and reminds us that God is at work, bringing beauty from ashes and purpose from pain. Joy is both a gift and a choice, a gift of God's Spirit and a decision to trust Him and praise Him, regardless of the circumstances.

Take a moment today to reflect on the joy of the Lord in your life. Where can you see His hand at work? How can you intentionally choose joy, even in the midst of challenges? Reimagined joy isn't about denying hardship; it's about embracing the truth that God is your source of strength and that His joy can carry you through anything.

Reflection Questions:

1. What is the difference between joy in the Lord and happiness based on circumstances?

2. How can trusting in God's promises help you reclaim joy in difficult times?

3. What small blessings or moments of gratitude can you focus on today to cultivate joy?

4. How does the idea of joy as a source of strength encourage you to face life's challenges with hope?

Section Two

REIMAGINING PURPOSE

Examining how God refines and renews our sense of calling and direction in life.

DAY 9

REIMAGINED
CALLING

"He has saved us and called us to a holy calling, not because of our works but because of His own purpose and grace, which He gave us in Christ Jesus before the ages began."
— 2 Timothy 1:9

Your calling is not a random series of events or accomplishments, it is a holy invitation to partner with God in His plans for your life. In 2 Timothy 1:9, Paul reminds us that our calling is rooted in God's purpose and grace, not in our own efforts. Reimagined calling invites us to see our lives as part of God's eternal story, where every talent, experience, and opportunity is woven together for His glory and our good.

Understanding your calling begins with recognizing that it is not limited to a specific job or role. It's about who you are in Christ and how you live out His love and purpose each day. Reimagined calling challenges us to move beyond narrow definitions of success and embrace a life that reflects God's character and advances His kingdom. Whether you are leading a ministry, raising a family, or working in the marketplace, your calling is sacred and significant.

Reimagined calling also requires a heart of surrender. Too often, we pursue our own ambitions without seeking God's direction. But true fulfillment comes when we allow Him to guide our steps. This might mean stepping out in faith to follow a new path or staying faithful in a current season that feels ordinary. Trusting God with your calling means believing that He knows what is best and will equip you for the journey ahead.

In the challenges of pursuing your calling, God's grace sustains you. He never calls you to something without providing the strength and resources to carry it out. Reimagined calling is not about striving for perfection but about walking in obedience, even when the path is unclear. It's about leaning on His power, knowing that your weaknesses are opportunities for His strength to shine

Today, reflect on how you can reimagine your calling in light of God's purpose and grace. Are there areas where you need to surrender your plans and trust His direction? Reimagined calling reminds us that every day is an opportunity to live out the unique purpose God has designed for us. As you embrace this truth, you'll discover the joy and fulfillment of a life fully aligned with His will.

Reflection Questions:

1. How does viewing your calling as rooted in God's purpose and grace change your perspective on your life's work?

2. Are there areas where you are pursuing your own plans instead of seeking God's direction? How can you surrender them to Him?

3. How can you live out your calling in your current season, even if it feels ordinary or uncertain?

4. What steps of faith can you take today to embrace the holy calling God has placed on your life?

DAY 10

REIMAGINED
SERVICE

"The Son of Man did not come to be served, but to serve, and to give His life as a ransom for many."
— Matthew 20:28

Service is at the heart of Jesus' ministry. In Matthew 20:28, Jesus reminds us that His mission was not to be served, but to serve and to sacrifice for others. Reimagining service means seeing it not as an obligation or a chore, but as a profound way to reflect Christ's love and align us with God's heart. True service flows from a heart transformed by God's grace, seeking to bless others as we have been blessed by Him.

Serving others allows us to step outside of ourselves and embrace a purpose greater than personal gain. In a world that often prioritizes self-interest, Jesus models a life of humility and generosity. When we serve with His mindset, we grow closer to Him and deepen our understanding of what it means to love others unconditionally. Reimagined service isn't about grand gestures, it's about daily acts of kindness and faithfulness that reveal God's love to those around us.

Sometimes, we may feel like our service is small or insignificant, but God uses every act of obedience to make an impact. Whether it's a word of encouragement, helping a neighbor in need, or volunteering at church, each act of service is a way to share His light. Reimagining service helps us see the beauty in the everyday opportunities to serve. It reminds us that God values our willingness to give, regardless of the size of our offering.

Service also has the power to renew our own sense of purpose. When we serve others, we often find that our hearts are transformed in the process. It draws us closer to God's heart and reminds us that we are part of His greater plan. Reimagined service helps us move from asking, "What can I get?" to "What can I give?" This shift brings joy and fulfillment that only comes from living in alignment with God's will.

Take a moment to reflect on how you can serve in your current season of life. Whether you're in a position of leadership, caring for family, or simply looking for small ways to bless others, know that your service matters to God. Reimagined service invites us to follow Jesus' example, living lives of humility, generosity, and love. As we serve, we align ourselves with God's heart and make His love tangible to those around us.

Reflection Questions:

1. How does seeing service as a reflection of Christ's love change your perspective on serving others?

2. What opportunities do you have in your daily life to serve others, even in small ways?

3. Have you ever experienced joy or renewal from serving someone else? What did it teach you about God's heart?

4. How can you shift your focus from "What can I get?" to "What can I give?" in your relationships and community?

DAY 11

REIMAGINED
STEWARDSHIP

"As each has received a gift, use it to serve one another, as good stewards of God's varied grace."
— 1 Peter 4:10

Stewardship is about recognizing that everything we have; our time, talents, treasures, and even our bodies, ultimately belongs to God. 1 Peter 4:10 reminds us that the gifts we have received are not meant for our benefit alone but are entrusted to us to serve others and glorify God. Reimagining stewardship means embracing the responsibility of managing all that God has given us, including our physical health, in alignment with His purposes. When we steward our lives well, we reflect our gratitude for God's grace and His trust in us.

Our bodies, described in Scripture as temples of the Holy Spirit (1 Corinthians 6:19-20), are a vital part of our stewardship. Reimagining stewardship means viewing our health and well-being as an offering to God. Are we caring for our physical health in a way that honors Him? This isn't about striving for perfection but recognizing that a healthy body allows us to serve God and others more effectively. From getting enough rest to fueling our bodies with proper nutrition, these small acts of care are acts of worship when done with a heart surrendered to Him.

Time is another precious resource we are called to steward wisely. Life's busyness can often cause us to use time reactively rather than intentionally. Reimagining stewardship of time involves setting aside moments for prayer, studying God's Word, and building meaningful relationships. It's about using time not just for productivity but for purpose, investing in what will have eternal value. Stewarding our time well also includes allowing for rest and renewal so that we can give our best to God and His work.

Our talents and treasures are equally important areas of stewardship. God has uniquely gifted each of us with skills and abilities that can be used to reflect His grace and meet the needs of others. Reimagined stewardship asks,

"How can I use these gifts to bless others and advance God's kingdom?" Similarly, our financial resources are tools for building His kingdom. By giving generously and managing our finances wisely, we demonstrate trust in God as our provider and make an impact that echoes into eternity.

Today, reflect on the gifts God has entrusted to you; your body, time, talents, and treasures. Are you using them in ways that honor Him? Reimagined stewardship is not about achieving perfection but living intentionally, knowing that everything we have is a sacred trust. By caring for our physical health, prioritizing what matters, and sharing our resources, we align our lives with God's purposes. Let's be faithful stewards, remembering that every gift is an opportunity to glorify God and serve others.

Reflection Questions:

1. How are you currently caring for your body as a temple of the Holy Spirit? What changes could you make to honor God with your physical health?

2. How can you better steward your time to align with God's priorities, including moments for rest and renewal?

3. What specific talents or abilities has God given you, and how can you use them to serve others in this season?

4. How does viewing your finances and resources as tools for God's kingdom change the way you approach giving and spending?

DAY 12

Reimagined

WORK

"Whatever you do, work heartily, as for the Lord and not for men."
— Colossians 3:23

Work is often viewed as a necessity, a way to provide for our needs and meet our responsibilities. However, Colossians 3:23 invites us to reimagine work as something much deeper. Paul encourages believers to approach their tasks "heartily, as for the Lord," shifting our perspective to see work as an act of worship. Reimagined work is not defined by job titles or positions but by the heart behind what we do. Whether we are leading a company, working behind the scenes, or caring for our families, every task has the potential to glorify God when done with faithfulness and excellence.

When we see work as worship, it transforms mundane tasks into meaningful ones. The small, everyday things, sending an email, cleaning the house, or preparing a meal, become opportunities to honor God with diligence and gratitude. Reimagined work reminds us that God is present in every aspect of our lives, not just in church or ministry. When we dedicate our efforts to Him, our work becomes an offering, reflecting His character and bringing Him glory.

This perspective also brings purpose and joy into our labor, even when the work feels challenging or repetitive. Knowing that we are ultimately serving God rather than people gives us a higher motivation to persevere and give our best. It helps us to find contentment in our work, recognizing that the value of what we do is not measured by worldly success but by our faithfulness to God's call in each season of life.

Reimagining work also includes reflecting Christ in our workplace relationships. Whether it's through integrity, kindness, or going the extra mile, our actions can point others to God. Work becomes a mission field where we can demonstrate God's love and excellence to those around us. Even in difficult environments, our commitment to working for the Lord can influence and inspire others, showing them a different way of living and serving.

EMBRACING CHANGE

Take time today to consider how you view your daily work. Are you approaching it with a heart that seeks to honor God? Reimagined work is not about striving for perfection but about offering your best to Him in all that you do. When we shift our focus from earthly rewards to eternal significance, our work becomes an act of worship, transforming the way we see every task and every opportunity.

Reflection Questions:

1. How does viewing work as worship change the way you approach your daily tasks, whether big or small?

2. In what ways can you dedicate your work to God, even in challenging or mundane moments?

3. How can you reflect Christ in your workplace relationships or interactions with others?

4. What steps can you take to find greater purpose and joy in your work by seeing it as a way to serve the Lord?

DAY 13

REIMAGINED
CREATIVITY

"And He has filled him with the Spirit of God, with skill, intelligence, and knowledge in all craftsmanship, to devise artistic designs."
— Exodus 35:31-32

Creativity is a gift from God, deeply rooted in His character. In Exodus 35:31-32, we see that God filled Bezalel with His Spirit, granting him the skill and intelligence to create beautiful and intricate designs for the tabernacle. This passage reminds us that creativity is not limited to artistic expression; it's a reflection of God's image in us. Reimagining creativity means recognizing that every one of us has been given the ability to create, whether through art, words, problem-solving, or innovation, to glorify God and bring beauty into the world.

When we embrace our creativity, we mirror God as the ultimate Creator. Just as He created the heavens and the earth with intention and beauty, He calls us to use our skills to enhance and reflect His glory. This creativity might show up in unexpected ways: designing a solution at work, crafting a meal for your family, or writing words that encourage someone's heart. Reimagined creativity asks us to expand our view and see every opportunity to create as an act of worship that reveals God's brilliance.

Creativity is not reserved for the "naturally gifted." Just as Bezalel was empowered by God's Spirit, we are equipped by Him to use our unique gifts for His purposes. You don't have to be a painter or a musician to be creative. Whether you are leading a team, organizing a space, or coming up with new ideas, your creativity is a reflection of God's work in you. It's not about being perfect but about being willing to let God inspire and guide your efforts.

Reimagined creativity also has the power to transform the world around us. When we use our gifts to serve others and share the beauty of God's love, we bring light into darkness and hope into despair. Whether it's through art, hospitality, writing, or innovation, God uses our creative efforts to bless others and reveal His goodness. By stepping into our creative callings, we join Him in the work of renewal and restoration.

Take a moment today to reflect on the unique ways God has made you creative. How can you use your creativity to glorify Him and bless others? Reimagined creativity is not about competition or comparison but about embracing the gifts God has given you and using them with boldness. When you allow His Spirit to work through you, your creativity becomes a powerful testimony of His presence in your life.

Reflection Questions:

1. How does recognizing creativity as a reflection of God's image change the way you view your own gifts and abilities?

2. In what areas of your life, whether at work, home, or church, can you use creativity to glorify God?

3. Have you ever experienced God working through your creativity to encourage or bless someone else? What was that experience like?

4. How can you overcome fear, perfectionism, or comparison to step boldly into the creative gifts God has given you?

DAY 14

REIMAGINED
LEADERSHIP

~~~~

*"But whoever would be great among you
must be your servant."*
— Matthew 20:26

Leadership, in the world's eyes, is often associated with power, authority, and recognition. However, Jesus redefines leadership in Matthew 20:26, calling His followers to lead through service. Reimagining leadership means rejecting the idea of status-driven authority and embracing a model of humility, love, and care for others. True leadership mirrors Christ, who demonstrated His greatness not by demanding service but by humbling Himself and serving others, even to the point of washing His disciples' feet.

At its core, reimagined leadership is about putting others first. A servant-leader prioritizes the needs, growth, and well-being of those they lead. Whether you're in a formal leadership position or simply influencing others in your daily life, leadership becomes an opportunity to reflect Christ's heart. It's about listening, encouraging, and lifting others up, rather than seeking personal gain or recognition. When we lead with humility, we demonstrate a love that builds trust and inspires others to follow God's example.

Jesus shows us that leadership is not about what we can get from others but what we can give. Reimagined leadership might mean going the extra mile to help someone struggling, showing patience when others make mistakes, or taking responsibility for difficult situations with grace. It's not always glamorous, but it's deeply impactful. When we lead in this way, we reflect the character of Christ, who gave everything for the people He came to save.

This kind of leadership requires strength, humility, and reliance on God. Leading as a servant often means putting aside our preferences, pride, or need for control to do what is best for others. It's a call to lead with compassion and integrity, trusting that God's approval matters more than the world's applause. As we follow

Christ's example, we can lead with confidence, knowing that His Spirit equips us for the task and uses our efforts for His glory.

Take some time today to reflect on how you approach leadership. Whether you are leading in your family, workplace, church, or community, reimagined leadership asks you to consider how you can serve others more intentionally. When you lead with humility and love, you not only reflect Christ's heart but also inspire those around you to live and lead in the same way.

Reflection Questions:

1. How does Jesus' example of servant-leadership challenge the way you view leadership?

2. In what areas of your life are you called to lead, and how can you model humility and service in those roles?

3. What barriers, such as pride, fear, or a desire for recognition, might prevent you from leading as a servant?

4. How can leading with a heart that mirrors Christ inspire and encourage those around you?

DAY 15

Reimagined

GOALS

~~~~

*"I press on toward the goal for the prize of the
upward call of God in Christ Jesus."*
— Philippians 3:14

Goals give our lives direction, providing something to strive for and a sense of purpose. However, Philippians 3:14 reminds us that as followers of Christ, our ultimate goal is not tied to earthly success but to the "prize of the upward call of God." Reimagining goals means aligning our ambitions with God's eternal purpose, allowing His will to shape our desires and pursuits. It's not about abandoning our dreams but inviting God into the process so that what we strive for reflects His glory and draws us closer to Him.

When we evaluate our goals in light of eternity, we realize that some of the things we chase may hold little lasting value. Achievements, accolades, and possessions can bring temporary satisfaction but cannot fulfill the deeper longing for purpose and meaning. Reimagined goals shift our focus from fleeting rewards to the things that truly matter, loving God, serving others, and living a life that reflects Christ. These goals bring not only fulfillment but also eternal impact.

Reimagining goals doesn't mean we stop setting practical objectives, such as career advancement, financial stability, or personal growth. Instead, it challenges us to ask deeper questions: How does this goal honor God? Does it align with His purpose for my life? For example, pursuing a career might not just be about personal success but about creating opportunities to serve and influence others for Christ. When we set goals with God's perspective, they become acts of worship and obedience, not just personal achievements.

This shift in perspective also helps us persevere when challenges arise. When our goals are rooted in God's will, we trust that He is working even when progress seems slow or setbacks occur. Reimagined goals remind us that the process is as important as the outcome. God often uses the journey of pursuing a goal to refine our character, strengthen our faith, and draw us closer to Him. By keeping our eyes on the ultimate prize, our relationship with Christ, we can press on with hope and purpose.

Take a moment to reevaluate your current goals. Are they aligned with God's eternal purpose, or are they focused solely on earthly rewards? Reimagined goals invite us to let go of striving for things that don't last and to embrace ambitions that reflect God's heart. When we press on toward His calling, we experience not only His guidance but also the deep joy of living a life with eternal significance.

Reflection Questions:

1. How do your current goals reflect (or not reflect) God's eternal purpose for your life?

2. What practical steps can you take to align your ambitions with God's will and seek His guidance in your plans?

3. How can trusting God's timing and purpose help you persevere when your progress feels slow or uncertain?

4. What does "pressing on toward the prize" look like for you in this season of life?

DAY 16

Reimagined

SUCCESS

"This Book of the Law shall not depart from your mouth, but you shall meditate on it day and night, so that you may be careful to do according to all that is written in it. For then you will make your way prosperous, and then you will have good success."
— Joshua 1:8

Success is often defined by the world as the accumulation of wealth, recognition, and personal accomplishments. But in Joshua 1:8, God redefines success for His people, tying it not to worldly achievements but to faithfulness to His Word. True success, in God's eyes, comes from meditating on Scripture, living in obedience to His commands, and aligning our lives with His plan. Reimagined success is about shifting our focus from external rewards to the internal fulfillment that comes from walking faithfully with God.

When we view success through a worldly lens, it can lead to exhaustion, comparison, and discontentment. We chase after goals that may satisfy for a moment but leave us longing for more. However, reimagining success invites us to see it as a byproduct of faithfulness to God. When we prioritize obedience to His Word and seek to glorify Him in all we do, we experience a deeper, lasting fulfillment that the world cannot provide.

This doesn't mean that ambition or hard work is wrong. God calls us to use our talents, work diligently, and strive for excellence in everything we do. But reimagined success shifts the goalpost, it's not about how much we achieve but about how faithfully we pursue what God has called us to do. Whether we're leading a business, raising a family, or serving in ministry, success is measured by our willingness to follow God's lead and trust Him with the outcomes.

Reimagined success also frees us from the trap of comparison. When we define success by faithfulness to God, we recognize that each person's calling is unique. God's plan for your life will not look the same as someone else's, and that's okay. By focusing on obedience rather than outcomes, we can celebrate others' victories while remaining confident in our own path. Success becomes less about impressing others and more about pleasing God.

Take time today to reflect on how you define success. Are your goals rooted in worldly standards, or are they focused on faithfulness to God's plan? Reimagined success invites you to trust that when you prioritize His Word and follow His guidance, you will prosper in ways that truly matter. Let your measure of success be not in the applause of people but in the approval of the One who calls you His own.

Reflection Questions:

1. How does God's definition of success in Joshua 1:8 differ from the world's view of success?

2. In what areas of your life can you shift your focus from achieving worldly success to pursuing faithfulness to God?

3. How can meditating on God's Word and living in obedience shape your understanding of what it means to be successful?

4. What steps can you take to avoid comparison and instead embrace the unique calling God has placed on your life?

SECTION THREE

REIMAGINING FAITHFULNESS

Encouraging consistency and resilience in trusting God and walking with him daily.

DAY 17

REIMAGINED
PATIENCE

"Wait for the Lord; be strong, and let your heart take courage; wait for the Lord!"
— Psalm 27:14

Patience is one of the most challenging virtues to cultivate in a world driven by instant gratification. Psalm 27:14 reminds us that waiting on the Lord is not passive but an act of faith and strength. Reimagined patience invites us to see the waiting seasons of life not as wasted time but as opportunities to trust in God's perfect timing and grow in our reliance on Him. It's in the waiting that God shapes our character and prepares us for what lies ahead.

Trusting in God's timing requires us to release our need for control. Often, we want answers and solutions immediately, but God works according to His divine schedule, not ours. Reimagining patience means believing that His plans are worth waiting for, even when we don't understand the delay. It's a choice to trust that He is working behind the scenes, weaving every detail together for our good and His glory.

Patience also teaches us to focus on the present rather than anxiously looking ahead. When we are consumed by what we're waiting for, we can miss the blessings and lessons God has for us right now. Reimagined patience encourages us to find purpose in the waiting by seeking His presence, deepening our faith, and serving others. These moments are not about idleness but about preparation for what God is bringing next.

Waiting with patience also strengthens our courage and resilience. Psalm 27:14 calls us to "be strong" and "let your heart take courage" as we wait for the Lord. This doesn't mean suppressing our emotions or pretending the waiting is easy; it means leaning on God for the strength to endure. Reimagined patience gives us the confidence to stand firm in faith, trusting that His promises are worth holding onto, no matter how long it takes.

Today, consider an area of your life where you are waiting on God. What would it look like to reimagine this season of waiting as a time of growth and preparation? Patience is not about passively enduring; it's about actively trusting God's perfect timing. When we wait with faith and courage, we discover that He is faithful to fulfill His promises in ways that exceed our expectations.

Reflection Questions:

1 How does trusting in God's perfect timing change the way you view waiting seasons in your life?

2. In what ways can you find purpose and growth during times of waiting?

3. What current situation is challenging your patience, and how can you surrender it to God with trust?

4. How does leaning on God for strength and courage help you endure waiting with hope and peace?

DAY 18

REIMAGINED
RESILIENCE

"Count it all joy, my brothers, when you meet trials of various kinds, for you know that the testing of your faith produces steadfastness."
— James 1:2-3

Resilience is the ability to endure challenges and bounce back stronger, but as believers, it's more than just perseverance, it's about letting trials refine our faith and draw us closer to God. James 1:2-3 encourages us to view trials not as setbacks but as opportunities for growth. Reimagining resilience means seeing difficulties through the lens of faith, trusting that God uses them to strengthen us and equip us for the journey ahead.

Trials are inevitable in life, but they don't have to break us. Instead, they can build us. When we face hardship with faith, we develop steadfastness, a resilience that allows us to stand firm in God's promises. Reimagined resilience teaches us that trials are not punishments but tools in God's hands, shaping us into people who reflect His character. Each challenge we endure becomes a step in our transformation, preparing us for greater purposes in His plan.

Resilience also requires a shift in perspective. James challenges us to "count it all joy" when we face trials, not because the trials themselves are pleasant, but because of what they produce in us. This joy comes from knowing that God is with us in every challenge, guiding us and providing the strength we need to persevere. Reimagined resilience helps us focus not on the pain of the moment but on the growth and purpose that God is working through it.

In practical terms, resilience means clinging to God's Word, praying for His strength, and leaning on the support of others when life feels overwhelming. It's about trusting that God's grace is sufficient, even when circumstances are tough. Reimagined resilience doesn't ignore pain or pretend everything is fine, it acknowledges the difficulty but chooses to trust God's ability to bring beauty from brokenness.

Consider the trials you're facing right now. How might God be using them to strengthen your faith and build resilience for the future? Reimagined resilience is not about avoiding challenges but embracing them as opportunities to grow in your reliance on God. When we trust Him through the storms, we find that He is faithful to sustain us, and our faith becomes stronger for the journey ahead.

Reflection Questions:

1. How can viewing trials as opportunities for growth change the way you approach challenges in your life?

2. What does it mean to "count it all joy" in the face of hardship? How can you apply this perspective?

3. In what ways has God used past challenges to build resilience in your faith?

4. How can trusting in God's presence and purpose help you face trials with greater courage and hope?

DAY 19

REIMAGINED

TRUST

~~~

*"You keep him in perfect peace whose mind is
stayed on you, because he trusts in you."*
— Isaiah 226:3

Trust is easy when life feels predictable, but it becomes much harder in seasons of uncertainty. Isaiah 26:3 reminds us that true peace comes from anchoring our trust in God, not in our circumstances. Reimagining trust means shifting our focus from trying to control outcomes to resting in God's unwavering love and faithfulness. Even when the future feels unclear, we can experience His perfect peace by keeping our minds fixed on Him.

Uncertainty often stirs doubt, causing us to question God's plans or timing. But reimagined trust invites us to see uncertainty as an opportunity to deepen our reliance on Him. God doesn't promise that we'll always understand His ways, but He does promise His presence. Trusting in His love allows us to release our fears, knowing that His wisdom far exceeds our own. When we place our trust in God, we find rest in the knowledge that He is guiding every step of our journey.

Building trust in God requires intentionality. Isaiah points to the importance of keeping our minds "stayed" on God, remaining grounded in His Word, prayer, and truth. Reimagined trust grows when we consistently return to His promises, even when doubts creep in. The more we remind ourselves of who God is and what He has done, the more our faith is strengthened. Over time, we learn to trust His character more than our changing circumstances.

This trust doesn't mean life will be free of hardship, but it allows us to navigate difficulties with confidence and calm. Reimagining trust reframes challenges, helping us see them not as obstacles but as opportunities to witness God's faithfulness. As our trust deepens, our perspective shifts from worry to worship, and we begin to rest in His perfect peace, no matter what storms we face.

Today, take time to reflect on areas where trust feels difficult. Where is God calling you to release control and

EMBRACING CHANGE

lean into His unfailing love? Reimagined trust leads us to surrender, inviting God to work in ways beyond what we can imagine. As you trust Him more deeply, you will discover the peace and security that come from standing firm in His promises.

Reflection Questions:

1. What areas of your life feel hardest to trust God with right now?

2. How can keeping your mind "stayed" on God help you experience greater peace during uncertain times?

3. Can you recall a time when trusting God brought peace, even when circumstances were challenging?

4. What practical steps can you take to deepen your trust in God's unfailing love daily?

Your Half-Way There Keep Up The Great Work!

DAY 20

REIMAGINED
DISCIPLINE

~~~~

"For the moment all discipline seems painful rather than pleasant, but later it yields the peaceful fruit of righteousness to those who have been trained by it."
— Hebrews 12:11

Discipline often carries a negative connotation, bringing to mind correction or restriction. However, Hebrews 12:11 reframes discipline as a gift, an essential part of our spiritual growth. Reimagining discipline means viewing it not as punishment but as a process that shapes us into the image of Christ. Just as an athlete endures training to grow stronger, God uses discipline to refine our hearts, producing the "peaceful fruit of righteousness" in our lives.

God's discipline is rooted in His love for us. Just as a loving parent corrects a child for their benefit, God allows challenges, convictions, and course corrections to draw us closer to Him. This divine discipline stretches and strengthens us, aligning our hearts with His will. Reimagining discipline reminds us that every moment of correction or challenge is an opportunity for God to transform us, not a sign of His displeasure. His goal is always our growth, not our failure.

Spiritual disciplines, such as prayer, fasting, reading Scripture, and worship, are also vital to our faith journey. These practices require consistency and commitment, but they shape our character and deepen our intimacy with God. Reimagining discipline helps us see these routines not as duties but as pathways to peace and spiritual vitality. The more we invest in these disciplines, the more we experience God's presence and guidance in our daily lives.

While discipline may feel difficult or uncomfortable at times, the long-term reward is undeniable. The peace and righteousness that Hebrews 12:11 describes emerge as we persist in trusting God's process. Over time, discipline leads to greater resilience, self-control, and clarity in our walk with Christ. It strengthens our ability to resist temptation, endure hardships, and stay faithful in every season.

Reflect on the areas in your life where God may be inviting you to embrace discipline. Is there a habit to develop, a sin to confront, or a practice to renew? Reimagined discipline isn't about perfection but about consistently showing up, trusting that God is shaping you day by day. As you lean into His correction and cultivate spiritual practices, you will experience the peace and righteousness that come from a life aligned with His purpose.

Reflection Questions:

1. How can you begin to view discipline as a tool for growth rather than as punishment or restriction?

2. What spiritual disciplines (prayer, Bible study, fasting, etc.) do you feel God is calling you to strengthen in this season?

3. How have you experienced growth or peace in the past through God's discipline or correction?

4. In what areas of your life might God be inviting you to embrace new habits or let go of old patterns to draw closer to Him?

DAY 21

Reimagined
ENDURANCE

~~~~~

"And let us not grow weary of doing good, for in due season we will reap, if we do not give up."
— Galatians 6:9

Endurance is the quiet strength that keeps us moving forward when circumstances feel heavy and progress seems slow. In Galatians 6:9, Paul encourages believers to persist in doing good, reminding them that their faithfulness will eventually yield fruit. Reimagined endurance invites us to view perseverance not as a burdensome task but as an act of faith, trusting that God's timing is perfect and His promises will come to pass.

The temptation to give up often comes when results are not immediate. We may pour our energy into relationships, ministries, or personal growth, only to feel discouraged when change isn't visible. But endurance teaches us that growth often happens beneath the surface, unseen but essential. Just as a seed takes time to sprout, the good we invest in others and in our walk with God will bear fruit in the right season. Reimagined endurance keeps us grounded in hope, even when the harvest feels distant.

Endurance is not achieved by sheer willpower but by leaning on God's strength. On our own, it's easy to grow tired and disillusioned. However, when we draw from the well of God's grace and presence, He renews our energy and restores our passion for the work He has set before us. Reimagining endurance reminds us that perseverance is not about striving alone but about walking in step with the One who sustains us.

God often uses seasons of endurance to refine our character and deepen our dependence on Him. As we press on, we become more resilient, learning to trust in God's faithfulness even when circumstances seem unchanging. Each step of obedience, no matter how small, builds spiritual stamina that equips us for greater challenges ahead. Reimagined endurance transforms difficulties into opportunities for growth, reminding us that the process is as valuable as the outcome.

Take a moment today to reflect on areas where you may feel weary. Where is God calling you to keep going, even when progress seems slow? Reimagined endurance invites you to trust that your faithfulness matters. God sees every effort, and His promise is sure, you will reap a harvest in due time. Don't give up. Let endurance carry you forward, anchored in the hope that God's plans are unfolding, even now.

Reflection Questions:

1. In what areas of your life do you feel weary or tempted to give up? How does Galatians 6:9 encourage you to keep going?

2. How can you rely more on God's strength rather than your own when facing long seasons of endurance?

3. Can you recall a time when persistence in doing good eventually bore fruit? How did that experience shape your faith?

4. What small acts of faithfulness can you commit to today, trusting that they will contribute to the harvest God is preparing?

DAY 22

REIMAGINED
HOPE

~~~~

"May the God of hope fill you with all joy and peace in believing, so that by the power of the Holy Spirit you may abound in hope."
— Romans 15:13

Hope is a vital part of our faith, yet it can feel elusive in the face of challenges. Romans 15:13 reminds us that our hope is not dependent on circumstances but is rooted in God's promises and power. Reimagined hope shifts our focus from fleeting optimism to the unshakable assurance that God is faithful to fulfill what He has spoken. This hope is not a wishful feeling, but a confident expectation grounded in His character and His Word.

God is described as the "God of hope" in this passage, emphasizing that He is the ultimate source of all true hope. When we feel weary or uncertain, we can turn to Him to be filled with joy and peace. Reimagined hope is a gift from the Holy Spirit, who empowers us to trust in God even when the future is unclear. It's a hope that doesn't depend on our own strength but flows from the One who holds all things together.

Living with reimagined hope means looking beyond the immediate and trusting in God's eternal promises. It's easy to get discouraged when prayers seem unanswered or progress feels slow, but hope reminds us that God is always at work. His timeline may not match ours, but His plans are perfect. When we anchor our hope in Him, we can face difficulties with confidence, knowing that He is weaving everything together for our good and His glory.

This kind of hope also transforms how we live each day. When we trust in God's promises, we are freed from fear and despair, allowing us to approach life with joy and peace. Reimagined hope gives us the courage to step out in faith, knowing that God's power is at work within us. It encourages us to share His hope with others, pointing them to the source of true and lasting peace.

Take time today to reflect on where your hope is anchored. Are you trusting in temporary things, or are you placing your hope in the unchanging promises of

God? Reimagined hope invites you to rest in His faithfulness, knowing that He will do what He has said. As you trust Him more deeply, you will find your heart filled with joy and peace, abounding in hope through the power of the Holy Spirit.

Reflection Questions:

1. How does anchoring your hope in God's promises change the way you face challenges?

2. What specific promises of God bring you comfort and hope during difficult times?

3. How can trusting in the power of the Holy Spirit help you renew your hope daily?

4. In what ways can you share the hope of God with those around you who may feel discouraged or uncertain?

DAY 23

REIMAGINED
HEALING

~~~~~

*"He heals the brokenhearted and binds
up their wounds."*
— Psalms 147:3

Healing is a central part of God's work in our lives, touching every part of our being, our hearts, minds, and spirits. Psalm 147:3 assures us that God is not distant or indifferent to our pain; He is close and actively involved in restoring us. Reimagining healing means understanding that it's not just about physical recovery but also about the deep restoration of our inner selves. God's healing power goes beyond what we can see, bringing wholeness where brokenness once existed.

God's healing begins in the heart. Whether we are burdened by grief, disappointment, or past hurts, He invites us to bring our brokenness to Him. His love is gentle and restorative, binding up our wounds and giving us the strength to move forward. Reimagined healing doesn't ignore the pain we've experienced; instead, it acknowledges that God's presence transforms even the hardest circumstances into opportunities for growth and renewal.

Healing is also a journey, not always an instant event. There may be seasons where we feel like progress is slow or incomplete, but God's work is always ongoing. Reimagining healing helps us trust in His timing, knowing that He is working all things together for our good. During this process, we are invited to rely on His Word, prayer, and community to find encouragement and strength. Each step toward healing is a testament to His faithfulness.

Beyond personal restoration, God's healing also prepares us to extend His love to others. As we experience His healing touch, we become vessels of His grace, able to comfort and encourage those who are struggling. Reimagined healing reminds us that our stories, even the painful ones, can be used to bring hope and wholeness to others. In God's hands, nothing is wasted.

Take a moment today to invite God into the areas of your life that need healing. Whether it's a broken relationship, a wounded heart, or a weary mind, trust that His restoration brings true peace and wholeness. Reimagined healing is not just about fixing what is broken; it's about being made whole in the presence of the One who knows us completely and loves us unconditionally.

Reflection Questions:

1. What areas of your life heart, mind, or spirit, need God's healing touch today?

2. How can trusting in God's timing help you embrace the journey of healing rather than focusing solely on the outcome?

3. In what ways have you experienced God's healing in the past, and how does that give you hope for the future?

4. How can you share the healing you've received from God to encourage and uplift others in their struggles?

DAY 24

Reimagined
FORGIVNESS

---

*"Be kind to one another, tenderhearted, forgiving one
another, as God in Christ forgave you."*
— Ephesians 4:32

Forgiveness is one of the most transformative acts we can experience, yet it can also be one of the most difficult. Ephesians 4:32 reminds us that forgiveness is not just a command but a reflection of God's grace in our lives. Reimagining forgiveness means seeing it not as something we reluctantly give but as a gift that brings freedom and peace, to both ourselves and others. It is a way to reflect Christ's love and break the chains of bitterness and resentment.

At the heart of forgiveness is the example of Jesus. Through His sacrifice, He demonstrated unconditional love and offered forgiveness to us, even when we were undeserving. Reimagined forgiveness invites us to extend that same grace to others, letting go of the need for revenge or justice and trusting God to handle the outcomes. Forgiveness doesn't excuse wrong behavior, but it releases us from the burden of carrying anger and hurt.

Forgiveness is also a pathway to personal freedom. Holding onto grudges can weigh us down emotionally and spiritually, preventing us from experiencing the fullness of God's peace. When we forgive, we free ourselves from the grip of bitterness and create space for healing and restoration. Reimagined forgiveness reminds us that letting go is not about minimizing our pain but about prioritizing our well-being and faithfulness to God.

Receiving forgiveness is equally important. Sometimes, we struggle to accept the forgiveness God offers, believing our mistakes are too great. Yet, His grace is sufficient for all our failures. Reimagined forgiveness encourages us to accept His mercy with gratitude and to offer the same forgiveness to ourselves. When we live in the freedom of forgiveness, we are better able to love and serve others with a tender heart.

Today, reflect on any areas where forgiveness is needed in your life. Is there someone you need to forgive, or is there forgiveness you need to accept? Reimagined forgiveness is not a one-time act but a continual choice to live in the freedom and peace of God's grace. As you embrace forgiveness, you'll discover the joy and wholeness that come from living in harmony with His love.

Reflection Questions:

1. How does reflecting on God's forgiveness toward you help you extend forgiveness to others?

2. What burdens or resentments could you release today by choosing to forgive?

3. Why is it sometimes difficult to accept God's forgiveness for your own mistakes, and how can you trust in His grace?

4. How can living in the freedom of forgiveness deepen your relationships with others and with God?

Section Four

REIMAGINING LOVE

Living out God's love in deeper, fuller, more transformative ways.

DAY 25

REIMAGINED
LOVE FOR GOD

~~~~

"And He said to him, 'You shall love the Lord your God with all your heart and with all your soul and with all your mind.'"
— Matthew 22:37

Loving God is the foundation of our faith, yet it's easy for that love to become routine or overshadowed by the busyness of life. In Matthew 22:37, Jesus reminds us that loving God requires our whole being, our heart, soul, and mind. Reimagining love for God invites us to move beyond surface-level devotion and into a deeper, more intentional relationship. It's a call to make Him the central focus of every aspect of our lives.

To love God with all our heart means offering Him our deepest affections and aligning our desires with His will. It involves examining what truly holds our attention and asking whether our priorities reflect our love for Him. Reimagined love for God isn't just about feelings; it's about choosing to seek Him daily, even when emotions waver. This kind of love grows as we spend time in His presence, allowing His Word to shape our hearts.

Loving God with all our soul speaks to the spiritual connection we share with Him. It's about surrendering our entire selves to His purposes and trusting Him with every part of our lives. Reimagined love for God calls us to worship Him not just in church but in every moment, through our words, actions, and attitudes. This soul-deep love reflects our gratitude for His grace and our recognition of His sovereignty.

To love God with all our mind involves engaging our thoughts and intellect in our relationship with Him. Reimagined love means meditating on His Word, seeking His wisdom, and intentionally guarding our minds against distractions that pull us away from Him. When we love God with our minds, we allow His truth to guide our decisions and transform the way we think about ourselves and the world around us.

Take time today to reflect on how you can reimagine your love for God. Are there areas of your heart, soul, or mind that you've withheld from Him? Reimagined love invites you to offer your whole self to Him in gratitude and worship. As you deepen your love for God, you'll find that it transforms your priorities, your perspective, and your purpose, drawing you closer to the One who loves you completely.

Reflection Questions:

1. What does it mean to love God with all your heart, soul, and mind? How can you apply this in your daily life?

2. Are there any distractions or priorities that may be hindering your ability to fully love God?

3. How can you intentionally nurture your love for God through prayer, Scripture, and worship?

4. In what ways does deepening your love for God affect your relationships with others and your overall perspective on life?

DAY 26

REIMAGINED
LOVE FOR OTHERS

"A new commandment I give to you, that you love one another: just as I have loved you, you also are to love one another."
— John 13:34

Jesus' command to love others as He has loved us sets a high standard for how we approach our relationships. In John 13:34, Jesus challenges us to move beyond surface-level kindness and embrace a sacrificial, selfless love that reflects His heart. Reimagined love for others means putting their needs above our own, even when it's inconvenient or difficult. It's a love rooted in humility, grace, and the willingness to serve.

To love others as Jesus does, we must first understand the depth of His love. Jesus loved sacrificially, giving up His own comfort and life for our sake. Reimagined love calls us to reflect this same sacrificial nature in our relationships. This might mean offering forgiveness when it's undeserved, extending kindness when it's inconvenient, or simply being present for someone in their time of need. Love in action mirrors the heart of Christ and brings His light into the lives of others.

This kind of love also requires us to let go of pride and selfishness. It's easy to focus on our own needs and desires, but reimagined love calls us to prioritize the well-being of others. Putting others first doesn't mean neglecting ourselves; it means seeing their value through God's eyes and choosing to serve them in love. When we act out of selflessness, we reflect the heart of Jesus and create stronger, more meaningful relationships.

Reimagined love for others also includes showing grace in moments of conflict or misunderstanding. It's about choosing compassion over judgment and reconciliation over resentment. This love seeks to understand rather than to be understood, promoting peace and unity. When we love others as Christ loves us, we become instruments of His healing and restoration in our communities and families.

Take a moment to reflect on how you can reimagine love in your relationships. Where can you extend sacrificial love, grace, or forgiveness? Reimagined love for others is not about perfection but about consistently striving to reflect God's love in all that you do. As you love others with humility and compassion, you embody the heart of Christ and become a living testament to His transformative love.

Reflection Questions:

1. What does it mean to love others as Jesus has loved you? How can you apply this in your relationships?

2. In what areas of your life is God calling you to practice sacrificial or selfless love?

3. How can showing grace and compassion in moments of conflict reflect Christ's love to others?

4. How might loving others with humility and service strengthen your relationships and build unity?

DAY 27

Reimagined
COMPASSION

~~~~

*"Put on then, as God's chosen ones, holy and beloved,
compassionate hearts, kindness, humility,
meekness, and patience."*
— John 13:34

Compassion is more than just feeling sympathy for someone in need; it's about actively responding with kindness and care. Colossians 3:12 calls us, as God's chosen and beloved people, to clothe ourselves with compassion. Reimagining compassion means seeing others through the lens of God's grace, understanding their struggles, and responding in ways that reflect His love. It's about going beyond acknowledgment and stepping into action to meet the needs of those around us.

To cultivate a compassionate heart, we must first recognize how God has shown compassion to us. His mercy and grace are limitless, reaching us in our brokenness and offering us hope and restoration. Reimagined compassion invites us to extend the same grace to others, especially when it's undeserved. It's a love that goes beyond convenience, mirroring the kindness and humility of Christ, who consistently put others' needs before His own.

Compassion requires us to slow down and truly see others. In a fast-paced world, it's easy to overlook the pain and struggles of those around us. Reimagining compassion means taking the time to listen, empathize, and engage with others in meaningful ways. Whether it's offering a word of encouragement, lending a helping hand, or simply being present, small acts of compassion can make a profound impact.

Living with compassion also challenges us to confront our own biases and judgments. It calls us to see people as God sees them, valuable, loved, and worthy of dignity. Reimagined compassion breaks down barriers and fosters unity by reminding us that we are all recipients of God's grace. When we choose compassion over criticism, we create space for healing, understanding, and reconciliation in our relationships and communities.

Today, consider how you can embody compassion in your interactions. Are there opportunities to show kindness, patience, or humility to someone in need? Reimagined compassion isn't about grand gestures; it's about living each day with a heart that reflects God's love. As you cultivate this heart, you'll find that compassion not only blesses others but also deepens your connection with God and His purpose for your life.

Reflection Questions:

1. How has God's compassion toward you shaped your understanding of how to treat others?

2. What practical steps can you take to cultivate a heart of compassion in your daily life?

3. In what ways can slowing down and truly seeing others help you respond with kindness and care?

4. How can choosing compassion over judgment bring healing and unity to your relationships and community?

DAY 28

REIMAGINED
MERCY

"Blessed are the merciful, for they shall receive mercy."
— Matthew 5:7

Mercy is one of the most profound expressions of God's love and grace, and in Matthew 5:7, Jesus promises blessings to those who show mercy to others. Reimagined mercy calls us to go beyond simply forgiving, it invites us to actively extend compassion, kindness, and grace to those who may not deserve it. Mercy reflects God's own heart, reminding us that we, too, are recipients of His unending mercy.

To be merciful is to embody God's character. Through Christ, we have received forgiveness, grace, and kindness, even when we least deserved it. Reimagined mercy challenges us to offer the same to others, not as an obligation, but as a joyful response to what we have been given. When we show mercy, we demonstrate God's love in action, revealing His character to a world that often prioritizes judgment over compassion.

Mercy requires a willingness to let go of anger, resentment, or the desire for revenge. It's easy to hold onto offenses, but reimagined mercy calls us to release those burdens and choose forgiveness instead. This act of releasing not only frees the other person but also brings peace and healing to our own hearts. Mercy doesn't excuse wrongdoing but offers the opportunity for restoration and reconciliation.

Living with mercy also means being mindful of those who are struggling or vulnerable. Reimagined mercy compels us to extend kindness to those in need, whether through physical help, emotional support, or simply listening with care. In a world often quick to criticize or condemn, mercy provides a powerful witness to God's love. It bridges divides and creates opportunities for healing and connection.

Today, reflect on how mercy plays a role in your life. Is there someone you need to forgive or help? Reimagined mercy reminds us that as we extend grace and kindness to others, we open ourselves to receive more of God's mercy in return. Let mercy shape your relationships, your actions, and your heart, transforming the way you interact with others and reflect God's love in the world.

Reflection Questions:

1. How has God's mercy toward you shaped the way you view and treat others?

2. Is there someone in your life who needs your forgiveness or kindness? How can you extend mercy to them today?

3. What barriers, such as pride or resentment, might prevent you from showing mercy, and how can you overcome them?

4. How can practicing mercy create opportunities for healing and reconciliation in your relationships and community?

DAY 29

REIMAGINED
SACRIFICE

"I appeal to you therefore, brothers, by the mercies of God, to present your bodies as a living sacrifice, holy and acceptable to God, which is your spiritual worship."
— Romans 12:1

Sacrifice is often associated with loss, but in Romans 12:1, Paul calls believers to see it as an act of worship. Presenting our lives as a "living sacrifice" means giving every part of ourselves, our time, resources, and talents to God in devotion. Reimagined sacrifice is not about begrudgingly giving something up but joyfully offering ourselves in response to His overwhelming mercy and love. It's a way to reflect God's heart, as His greatest act of love was the sacrifice of His Son for us.

Sacrificial love is central to God's character. Jesus demonstrated this through His life and death, giving everything to redeem us. Reimagined sacrifice invites us to model this kind of love in our own lives, putting others before ourselves and seeking their well-being. Whether it's through acts of service, financial generosity, or offering time to someone in need, our sacrifices become a reflection of Christ's love.

Living sacrificially also shifts our focus from self-centeredness to God-centeredness. It requires us to let go of comfort, convenience, or personal ambition to pursue what matters most to Him. Reimagined sacrifice doesn't mean we must abandon all joy or rest; rather, it calls us to align our priorities with God's purposes. When we trust Him with our sacrifices, we find that He uses them to bring blessing and transformation, both in our lives and in the lives of others.

Sacrifice, though challenging, is deeply rewarding. It strengthens our faith, teaches us humility, and fosters deeper dependence on God. Each time we surrender something to Him, we experience the freedom and joy that come from walking in obedience. Reimagined sacrifice reminds us that God honors our offerings, no matter how small, and uses them to accomplish His greater plans.

Today, reflect on areas in your life where God may be calling you to sacrificial love. Are there opportunities to give of your time, talents, or resources for His glory? Reimagined sacrifice is not about what we lose but about what we gain, a closer relationship with God and a deeper understanding of His heart. As you offer yourself to Him, you'll discover the peace and fulfillment that come from living as a true reflection of His love.

Reflection Questions:

1. How does viewing sacrifice as worship change the way you approach giving your time, resources, or energy?

2. What is one area of your life where God may be calling you to sacrificial love?

3. How can modeling Jesus' sacrificial love strengthen your relationships and witness to others?

4. In what ways have you experienced joy or growth through sacrifices you've made for God or others?

DAY 30

REIMAGINED

PATIENCE IN LOVE

"Love is patient and kind; love does not envy or boast; it is not arrogant."
— 1 Corinthians 13:4

Patience is a defining quality of love, yet it's often the most challenging to practice, especially in relationships. In 1 Corinthians 13:4, Paul reminds us that love is patient and kind, emphasizing that true love endures with grace. Reimagined patience in love calls us to move beyond fleeting emotions and practice steadfastness, even when others test our limits. This kind of patience mirrors God's enduring love for us, which is never rushed, conditional, or easily exhausted.

EMBRACING CHANGE

Practicing patience in love means choosing to remain calm and gracious when faced with frustration or disappointment. It's about creating space for others to grow and make mistakes, just as God does for us. Reimagined patience invites us to extend understanding and grace in our relationships, rather than reacting out of anger or impatience. This kind of love builds trust and fosters deeper connections, allowing relationships to thrive even in difficult seasons.

Patience also requires us to let go of unrealistic expectations. No one is perfect, and reimagined patience acknowledges that growth and healing take time. Instead of focusing on what others aren't doing right, we can choose to celebrate small victories and progress. By shifting our perspective, we align our hearts with God's and allow His love to shape the way we respond to those around us.

This patience isn't passive; it's active and intentional. Reimagined patience means praying for those who challenge us, seeking God's guidance in moments of frustration, and looking for ways to show kindness even when it's hard. It requires strength and humility to choose love when it would be easier to walk away or hold a grudge. But as we lean on God for patience, He equips us with the ability to endure and love deeply, just as He does.

Take time today to reflect on the relationships in your life. Are there areas where patience is being tested? Reimagined patience in love challenges us to reflect God's heart, offering grace and understanding even in the midst of difficulty. As we practice this kind of love, we not only strengthen our relationships but also grow closer to God, who is the ultimate example of perfect patience.

Reflection Questions:

1. How does God's patience with you shape the way you approach patience in your relationships?

2. What are some practical ways you can extend patience and grace to others, especially when it's difficult?

3. Are there any unrealistic expectations in your relationships that you need to release to practice reimagined patience?

4. How can relying on God's strength help you show enduring love in challenging situations?

DAY 31

REIMAGINED
LOVE FOR ENEMIES

~~~~

"But I say to you, Love your enemies and pray for those who persecute you."
— Matthew 5:44

Loving our enemies goes against every instinct we have, yet it is one of Jesus' clearest and most challenging commands. In Matthew 5:44, Jesus calls us to love not just those who love us back but also those who wrong us, hurt us, or oppose us. Reimagined love for enemies requires a transformed heart, one that reflects God's grace and forgiveness. It's not about condoning wrongdoing but about choosing to rise above bitterness and extend the love that only God can provide.

This love starts with prayer. When we pray for those who hurt us, we invite God to soften our hearts and work in their lives. Prayer shifts our perspective, helping us see our enemies through God's eyes, as individuals made in His image, who are also in need of His grace. Reimagined love for enemies is rooted in humility, recognizing that just as we have received God's mercy, we are called to extend it to others, even when they seem undeserving.

Forgiveness is a vital part of loving our enemies. Holding onto anger or resentment only keeps us bound to the pain of the past. Reimagined love invites us to release those burdens, trusting God to bring justice and healing in His way and timing. Forgiveness doesn't mean ignoring hurt or allowing abuse; it means choosing to let go of the desire for revenge and allowing God to transform our hearts.

Loving our enemies is not a sign of weakness but of great spiritual strength. It takes courage and reliance on God to respond to hatred with love. Reimagined love for enemies empowers us to break the cycle of animosity and bring peace into our relationships and communities. It's a powerful witness to the transformative power of God's love, a love that can change hearts, including our own.

Today, ask God to help you reimagine how you view and respond to those who have wronged you. Are there areas where you need to extend forgiveness or pray for someone difficult in your life? Reimagined love for enemies is not something we can accomplish on our own; it requires God's strength and grace working in us. As you embrace this call, you'll discover the freedom and peace that come from loving as Christ loves.

Reflection Questions:

1. How does Jesus' example of loving His enemies, even on the cross, challenge your perspective on this command?

2. Who in your life might God be calling you to pray for or forgive, even if it feels difficult?

3. What steps can you take to let go of anger or resentment and allow God's love to transform your heart?

4. How can loving your enemies serve as a witness to God's grace and power to those around you?

DAY 32

REIMAGINED
UNITY IN LOVE

"With all humility and gentleness, with patience, bearing with one another in love, eager to maintain the unity of the Spirit in the bond of peace."
— Ephesians 4:2-3

Unity is a reflection of God's heart, and love is its foundation. In Ephesians 4:2-3, Paul urges believers to practice humility, gentleness, and patience, bearing with one another in love to preserve unity. Reimagined unity in love goes beyond surface-level agreement; it invites us to embrace diversity, resolve conflicts with grace, and prioritize relationships over personal preferences. This unity isn't something we achieve on our own, it's a work of the Holy Spirit as we commit to loving one another as Christ loves us.

Unity in love begins with humility. It requires us to set aside pride and self-centeredness, recognizing that others' perspectives and experiences are valuable. Reimagined unity calls us to approach one another with a willingness to listen, learn, and empathize. It's about valuing relationships over being "right" and seeking ways to build bridges rather than walls. In this posture, love becomes the glue that holds families, churches, and communities together.

Patience and gentleness are essential for unity. Relationships often involve misunderstandings and disagreements, but reimagined unity reminds us to respond with grace rather than frustration. Bearing with one another in love means extending compassion and forgiveness, even when it's difficult. It's a commitment to work through challenges together, trusting that God's Spirit is at work in each person, shaping us into His likeness.

Reimagined unity in love also means actively pursuing peace. It's not enough to avoid conflict; we are called to be peacemakers, addressing issues with honesty and love. This requires courage and a commitment to seeking reconciliation rather than letting division fester. When we prioritize unity, we reflect God's desire for His people to live in harmony, showing the world the power of His love through our actions.

Today, consider how you can embrace reimagined unity in your relationships. Are there areas where pride or unresolved conflict may be hindering unity? Love is the foundation that makes unity possible, but it requires intentional effort and reliance on the Holy Spirit. As you practice humility, gentleness, and patience, you'll contribute to a bond of peace that glorifies God and blesses those around you.

Reflection Questions:

1. How does practicing humility, gentleness, and patience help foster unity in your relationships?

2. Are there any conflicts or misunderstandings in your family, church, or community where you can take steps toward reconciliation?

3. How can you bear with others in love, especially when their actions or opinions differ from your own?

4. In what ways does unity within the body of Christ serve as a witness to God's love and power in the world?

Section Five

REIMAGINING THE FUTURE

*Embracing God's Vision for Your Future
with Hope, Trust, and Boldness*

DAY 33

REIMAGINED
DREAMS

─────

*"For I know the plans I have for you, declares the Lord,
plans for welfare and not for evil, to give you a
future and a hope."*
— Jeremiah 29:11

Dreams often reflect our hopes, ambitions, and desires, but as followers of Christ, we are invited to reimagine our dreams in light of God's greater purpose. Jeremiah 29:11 reminds us that God's plans for us are good, offering a future filled with hope. Reimagined dreams call us to surrender our personal ambitions to God and trust Him to shape our desires and goals according to His will. It's not about giving up on dreaming but about aligning our dreams with His perfect plans.

God's dreams for us are often bigger than we can imagine, yet they require trust and faith. Reimagining our dreams involves letting go of control and allowing God to guide the process. This may mean embracing unexpected paths or rethinking goals that don't align with His purpose for our lives. When we surrender our dreams to God, we discover that His plans not only fulfill our desires but also bring glory to His name.

Sometimes, reimagining dreams means holding onto hope even when life takes unexpected turns. Unfulfilled or delayed dreams can lead to frustration or discouragement, but God uses these seasons to grow our faith and prepare us for what's ahead. Reimagined dreams remind us that God's timing is perfect, and even when we don't see the full picture, we can trust that He is working all things together for good.

Reimagined dreams are also about impact. Instead of focusing solely on personal success or comfort, God invites us to dream in ways that bless others and advance His kingdom. This could mean pursuing a career that serves others, using our talents to glorify Him, or stepping out in faith to follow a calling that seems daunting. When our dreams are rooted in love for God and others, they become powerful tools for transformation and hope.

Take a moment to reflect on your dreams. Are they shaped by God's purposes, or are they rooted in personal ambition? Reimagined dreams challenge us to place our hopes and desires in God's hands, trusting Him to do more than we could ask or imagine. As you surrender your dreams to Him, you'll find that He leads you toward a future filled with joy, purpose, and eternal significance.

Reflection Questions:

1. How does surrendering your dreams to God change the way you approach your hopes and goals?

2. Are there any dreams you've held onto that may need to be reimagined to align with God's purpose for your life?

3. How has God's timing shaped your understanding of dreams that have been delayed or redirected?

4. In what ways can your dreams be used to bless others and advance God's kingdom?

DAY 34

REIMAGINED
PURPOSE IN UNCERTAINTY

*"The heart of man plans his way,
but the Lord establishes his steps."*
— Proverbs 16:9

Uncertainty can make us feel lost or stagnant, yet it's often in these seasons that God does His deepest work in us. Proverbs 16:9 reminds us that while we may have our plans, it is God who ultimately directs our steps. Reimagined purpose in uncertainty invites us to trust that God is still at work, even when the path ahead is unclear. Instead of feeling paralyzed by the unknown, we can lean into His guidance, knowing He is faithful to lead us.

Reimagined purpose in uncertainty requires a shift in perspective. Rather than focusing on what we can't control, we're invited to see every moment as an opportunity to grow and serve. Purpose isn't limited to grand achievements or long-term goals; it can be found in the small, faithful steps we take each day. Whether it's showing kindness, deepening our prayer life, or serving others, these acts of faith build a foundation for God's greater plans.

Trusting God in uncertainty also means surrendering our need for immediate answers. It's natural to want clarity and direction, but reimagined purpose asks us to walk by faith, not by sight. God often uses uncertain times to teach us reliance on Him, shaping our character and preparing us for what's ahead. In these moments, His purpose isn't just about what we accomplish but about who we become.

Uncertainty can also create space for God to reveal new possibilities. When our plans are disrupted, we are more open to seeing opportunities we might have overlooked. Reimagined purpose invites us to embrace this flexibility, trusting that God's detours are part of His perfect design. He is always working behind the scenes, using even the unknown to fulfill His promises and glorify His name.

Take time today to reflect on how you can embrace purpose, even in seasons of uncertainty. Are there small steps of faithfulness you can take right now? Reimagined purpose reminds us that God's plans are never stalled, even when ours seem to be. As you trust Him with the unknown, you'll discover that He is not only leading you but also using this season to draw you closer to Him and prepare you for what's next.

Reflection Questions:

1. How does trusting God to establish your steps change the way you approach uncertainty?

2. What small, faithful actions can you take today to live with purpose, even without clarity about the future?

3. How has God used past seasons of uncertainty to shape your character or reveal new opportunities?

4. How can focusing on God's presence and promises bring peace and purpose during uncertain times?

DAY 35

REIMAGINED
RISK

~~~~~

"He said, 'Come.' So Peter got out of the boat and walked on the water and came to Jesus."
— Matthew 14:29

Taking risks can be intimidating, but as believers, we are called to step out in faith when God invites us. In Matthew 14:29, Peter took a bold risk by stepping out of the boat to walk toward Jesus on the water. Reimagined risk is not about reckless decisions but about trusting God when He calls us into the unknown. It's about moving beyond comfort zones and embracing opportunities to grow, serve, and follow His leading.

Reimagined risk begins with recognizing that faith often requires action. Like Peter, we must be willing to leave the safety of the familiar to experience the

extraordinary. This may mean pursuing a new ministry, mending a broken relationship, or sharing your faith in a difficult situation. While the outcome isn't guaranteed, reimagined risk reminds us that obedience to God is always worth it. When we step out in faith, we not only grow but also witness God's power in new and transformative ways.

Taking risks for God also deepens our dependence on Him. Peter's journey on the water was sustained only by his focus on Jesus. When he doubted, he began to sink, but even then, Jesus was there to rescue him. Reimagined risk teaches us that it's not about having all the answers or guarantees, it's about keeping our eyes on Christ, trusting that He will guide and uphold us, even when the waves feel overwhelming.

Reimagined risk also involves releasing the fear of failure. It's easy to avoid stepping out because of the "what ifs," but God doesn't measure success the way the world does. He values faithfulness over results. Whether the risk leads to triumph or lessons learned, God uses every step of obedience for His glory and our growth. Each risk taken in faith strengthens our courage and prepares us for even greater acts of trust.

Today, consider what risks God may be calling you to take. Is there an area of your life where you've been

EMBRACING CHANGE

hesitant to step out in faith? Reimagined risk invites you to trust God's leading and embrace the opportunities He places before you. As you take those steps, you'll discover that God is not only with you but also working through you in ways that exceed your expectations.

Reflection Questions:

1. What does Peter's step of faith in Matthew 14:29 teach you about trusting God in risky situations?

2. Are there areas in your life where fear of failure is holding you back from stepping out in faith? How can you release that fear?

3. How can keeping your focus on Jesus help you take bold steps of obedience, even when the outcome is uncertain?

4. What is one risk God may be calling you to take, and how can you trust Him to guide and sustain you in the process?

DAY 36

REIMAGINED
REST

~~~~

*"Come to me, all who labor and are heavy laden,
and I will give you rest."*
— Matthew 11:28

Taking risks can be intimidating, but as believers, we are called to step out in faith when God invites us. In Matthew 14:29, Peter took a bold risk by stepping out of the boat to walk toward Jesus on the water. Reimagined risk is not about reckless decisions but about trusting God when He calls us into the unknown. It's about moving beyond comfort zones and embracing opportunities to grow, serve, and follow His leading.

Reimagined risk begins with recognizing that faith often requires action. Like Peter, we must be willing to leave the safety of the familiar to experience the

extraordinary. This may mean pursuing a new ministry, mending a broken relationship, or sharing your faith in a difficult situation. While the outcome isn't guaranteed, reimagined risk reminds us that obedience to God is always worth it. When we step out in faith, we not only grow but also witness God's power in new and transformative ways.

Taking risks for God also deepens our dependence on Him. Peter's journey on the water was sustained only by his focus on Jesus. When he doubted, he began to sink, but even then, Jesus was there to rescue him. Reimagined risk teaches us that it's not about having all the answers or guarantees, it's about keeping our eyes on Christ, trusting that He will guide and uphold us, even when the waves feel overwhelming.

Reimagined risk also involves releasing the fear of failure. It's easy to avoid stepping out because of the "what ifs," but God doesn't measure success the way the world does. He values faithfulness over results. Whether the risk leads to triumph or lessons learned, God uses every step of obedience for His glory and our growth. Each risk taken in faith strengthens our courage and prepares us for even greater acts of trust.

Today, consider what risks God may be calling you to take. Is there an area of your life where you've been hesitant to step out in faith? Reimagined risk invites you to trust God's leading and embrace the opportunities He places before you. As you take those steps, you'll discover that God is not only with you but also working through you in ways that exceed your expectations.

Reflection Questions:

1. What does Peter's step of faith in Matthew 14:29 teach you about trusting God in risky situations?

2. Are there areas in your life where fear of failure is holding you back from stepping out in faith? How can you release that fear?

3. How can keeping your focus on Jesus help you take bold steps of obedience, even when the outcome is uncertain?

4. What is one risk God may be calling you to take, and how can you trust Him to guide and sustain you in the process?

DAY 37

REIMAGINED
CONTENTMENT

~~~~~~

"I know how to be brought low, and I know how to abound. In any and every circumstance, I have learned the secret of facing plenty and hunger, abundance and need."
— Philippians 4:12

Taking risks can be intimidating, but as believers, we are called to step out in faith when God invites us. In Matthew 14:29, Peter took a bold risk by stepping out of the boat to walk toward Jesus on the water. Reimagined risk is not about reckless decisions but about trusting God when He calls us into the unknown. It's about moving beyond comfort zones and embracing opportunities to grow, serve, and follow His leading.

Reimagined risk begins with recognizing that faith often requires action. Like Peter, we must be willing to leave the safety of the familiar to experience the

extraordinary. This may mean pursuing a new ministry, mending a broken relationship, or sharing your faith in a difficult situation. While the outcome isn't guaranteed, reimagined risk reminds us that obedience to God is always worth it. When we step out in faith, we not only grow but also witness God's power in new and transformative ways.

Taking risks for God also deepens our dependence on Him. Peter's journey on the water was sustained only by his focus on Jesus. When he doubted, he began to sink, but even then, Jesus was there to rescue him. Reimagined risk teaches us that it's not about having all the answers or guarantees, it's about keeping our eyes on Christ, trusting that He will guide and uphold us, even when the waves feel overwhelming.

Reimagined risk also involves releasing the fear of failure. It's easy to avoid stepping out because of the "what ifs," but God doesn't measure success the way the world does. He values faithfulness over results. Whether the risk leads to triumph or lessons learned, God uses every step of obedience for His glory and our growth. Each risk taken in faith strengthens our courage and prepares us for even greater acts of trust.

Today, consider what risks God may be calling you to take. Is there an area of your life where you've been hesitant to step out in faith? Reimagined risk invites you to trust God's leading and embrace the opportunities He places before you. As you take those steps, you'll discover that God is not only with you but also working through you in ways that exceed your expectations.

Reflection Questions:

1. What does Peter's step of faith in Matthew 14:29 teach you about trusting God in risky situations?

2. Are there areas in your life where fear of failure is holding you back from stepping out in faith? How can you release that fear?

3. How can keeping your focus on Jesus help you take bold steps of obedience, even when the outcome is uncertain?

4. What is one risk God may be calling you to take, and how can you trust Him to guide and sustain you in the process?

DAY 38

REIMAGINED
CONVERSATIONS

*"Let your speech always be gracious, seasoned
with salt, so that you may know how
you ought to answer each person."*
— Colossians 4:6

Conversations are powerful tools that can either build others up or tear them down. In Colossians 4:6, Paul calls us to reimagine our speech, encouraging us to approach every conversation with grace and thoughtfulness. Reimagined conversations reflect Christ's love and wisdom, transforming our words into a source of encouragement, healing, and connection. They invite us to be intentional about how we communicate, making our words a reflection of God's character.

Reimagining conversations begins with grace. This means speaking in ways that uplift others, even in challenging or tense situations. Grace-filled conversations don't shy away from truth, but they deliver it with kindness and respect. Whether offering encouragement, resolving conflict, or sharing the gospel, our words should always be rooted in love and a desire to reflect God's heart.

Paul also encourages us to let our speech be "seasoned with salt," adding depth and meaning to our conversations. Reimagined conversations go beyond surface-level small talk to address matters of the heart. They involve listening actively, asking thoughtful questions, and being present with those we engage. When we approach conversations with intention and care, they become opportunities to share God's truth and build genuine relationships.

Reimagined conversations also call us to respond wisely. Each person we interact with has unique experiences and needs, requiring us to rely on the Holy Spirit for discernment. By praying for guidance and seeking God's wisdom, we can offer the right words at the right time. This intentionality allows our conversations to be both impactful and Christ-centered, drawing others closer to Him.

Today, consider how you can reimagine your conversations to reflect grace and purpose. Are there words you need to offer in encouragement or apologies you need to make? Reimagined conversations remind us that our speech is not just communication but a way to glorify God. As you approach each interaction with kindness, wisdom, and love, you'll find that your words have the power to bring life and transformation to those around you.

Reflection Questions:

1. How can letting your speech be gracious and "seasoned with salt" change the way you approach difficult conversations?

2. In what ways can you use your words to encourage and uplift others today?

3. How can listening actively and relying on the Holy Spirit improve the depth and impact of your conversations?

4. Are there any conversations you need to reimagine, whether by offering grace, speaking truth in love, or seeking reconciliation?

DAY 39

REIMAGINED
VISION

---

*"And the Lord answered me: 'Write the vision;
make it plain on tablets, so he may run who reads it.'"*
— Habakkuk 2:2

Vision is a vital part of our spiritual journey, giving us direction and clarity about God's purpose for our lives. In Habakkuk 2:2, God instructs the prophet to write the vision clearly so it can guide others. Reimagined vision invites us to see beyond the immediate and align our focus with God's eternal perspective. It's about asking Him to reveal His plans for our lives and trusting Him to lead us step by step toward His greater purpose.

Reimagined vision begins with seeking God's guidance. Instead of relying solely on our own understanding, we are called to prayerfully ask, "Lord, what do You want me to see?" This shift helps us focus on His plans rather than our own ambitions. As we reimagine our vision, we learn to see our lives through the lens of faith, recognizing that God's plans are always for our good and His glory.

This vision is not limited to personal goals; it includes how we serve and impact others. Reimagined vision reminds us to consider how our actions and choices align with God's kingdom purposes. Whether in our families, workplaces, or communities, we are invited to dream beyond ourselves and embrace a vision that blesses those around us. This broader perspective helps us live with intentionality, knowing that our lives can have eternal impact.

Reimagining vision also requires patience and perseverance. God's plans often unfold gradually, and it can be tempting to grow weary or lose focus. However, writing the vision "plain on tablets" reminds us to stay grounded in His promises, even when progress feels slow. Trusting His timing allows us to move forward with confidence, knowing He is faithfully working behind the scenes.

Take time today to reflect on the vision God has placed in your heart. Are you allowing Him to shape and refine it, or are you holding onto your own plans?

EMBRACING CHANGE

Reimagined vision invites you to surrender your perspective to God's and trust Him to lead you. As you align your vision with His, you'll find clarity, purpose, and the joy of walking in His perfect will.

Reflection Questions:

1. How does seeking God's guidance change the way you approach your vision and goals for the future?

2. In what ways can your vision reflect God's kingdom purposes and bless others?

3. What challenges or doubts might be hindering you from fully embracing the vision God has for your life?

4. How can trusting God's timing help you stay faithful and focused as His plans for your life unfold?

You Made It To The End!

DAY 40

Reimagined
VICTORY

"No, in all these things we are more than conquerors through Him who loved us."
— Romans 8:37

Victory in life is often thought of as achieving success, overcoming obstacles, or reaching personal goals. However, in Romans 8:37, Paul reveals a deeper and eternal perspective: true victory is found in Christ, who has already conquered sin and death for us. Reimagined victory is not about striving in our own strength but about living a life fully surrendered to God, trusting that His love and power make us "more than conquerors." This victory is not fleeting; it is eternal and unshakable.

Reimagined victory begins with surrender. It may seem counterintuitive, but the path to triumph in God's kingdom involves letting go of our need for control and allowing Him to lead. By aligning our hearts with His will, we experience a victory that is far greater than anything we could achieve on our own. This victory transcends circumstances, giving us confidence and peace even in the face of challenges.

This triumph is rooted in God's love. Romans 8 assures us that nothing can separate us from the love of Christ, not hardship, persecution, or even death. Reimagined victory reminds us that our worth and security are not tied to external successes but are anchored in God's unchanging love. When we live from this place of assurance, we can face life's trials with courage, knowing that the ultimate battle has already been won.

Living in reimagined victory also transforms how we approach life's struggles. Instead of being overwhelmed by difficulties, we can see them as opportunities to trust God more deeply and to grow in faith. This perspective shifts our focus from what we cannot control to what God is doing in and through us. It allows us to celebrate even small victories, knowing that they are part of a larger story of God's redemption and grace.

As you reflect on this final day of your devotional journey, take time to celebrate the victory you have in Christ. Are there areas where you need to surrender control or trust Him more fully? Reimagined victory is not about achieving perfection but about walking daily in the confidence of God's love and faithfulness. As you live a life fully surrendered to Him, you'll discover the joy and freedom that come from being more than a conqueror through Christ.

Reflection Questions:

1. How does Romans 8:37 change your understanding of what it means to live victoriously?

2. In what areas of your life do you need to surrender control to experience God's ultimate victory?

3. How does knowing that nothing can separate you from God's love give you confidence in the face of challenges?

4. What small victories in your life can you celebrate today as part of God's larger plan for you?

About the Author

Andre McCloud is a seasoned pastor, chaplain, and author with a deep passion for guiding others on their spiritual journeys. With years of experience as a senior pastor and former lay pastor, He has dedicated his life to teaching, encouraging, and inspiring people to embrace their faith and live out God's purpose in their lives. His work as a chaplain has provided him with unique insights into walking alongside individuals through life's challenges, offering hope and spiritual care in moments of need.

An accomplished author, Andre McCloud combines biblical wisdom with practical applications to help readers grow in their relationship with God. His compassionate leadership and heartfelt writing reflect a commitment to helping others find renewal, purpose, and transformation through God's Word. Whether speaking from the pulpit or writing for the page, he seeks to encourage believers to reimagine their lives in the light of God's love and grace.